moonflower

sabina laura

Copyright © Sabina Laura
All rights reserved.

No portion of this book may be used or
reproduced without written permission from
the author except for the use of brief
quotation in book reviews or scholarly
journals.

Cover design by Mitch Green
Words and illustrations by Sabina Laura

ISBN: 9781707239849

*this is for anyone trying to grow
through darkness.*

wilt *1*

grow *65*

bloom *129*

wilt

how beautifully
fragile
we are
that we accept pain
when we think
we deserve it
and let it break us
silently.

my bones are crushing
with the weight
of your absence
the two conflicting worlds
fighting inside of me
another day of trying to
let go
another night of wishing
you were here
and all the deepest,
darkest corners
of my mind
intoxicated
and tired of searching
for something
that i can't reach.

i spend my days dreaming
and my nights wide awake,
i live in yesterday
and speak in *i'm sorry*
because even when
my smile says sunshine
my eyes say
with a chance of rain.

i have been
dreaming in
constellations
but no matter
how many stars
i connect
the bigger picture
never becomes clear.

we broke away
from each other
like clouds
after a storm
but the sun never
reappeared for me
and i don't know
what to do
with all this rain.

winter is here
and in my heart
covering the wild in frost
and i cannot help but feel like
something has been lost.

they told me
to take everything
"with a pinch of salt"
but they didn't tell me
it would feel
like it was being
rubbed into my wounds.

there is dirt
buried beneath this skin.
there are days where
i want to tear it apart
and scrub it clean.

i wear my heart
on my sleeve
and no part of me remains
untouched.
sometimes,
it's too much.

it gets easier, they say
and i pretend
to be braver than i feel
but in truth,
there are some wounds
that time simply
cannot heal.

these words paint
a thousand pictures
but not enough to tell a story
and not enough
to build a home
but sometimes we spend
so long within walls
that they forget how to hold us
and we forget
how it feels to breathe.

like wildflowers trampled
by hurried footsteps,
trust is such a fragile thing.

so delicate.
so *breakable.*

it is sad
when i think about it —

how much kindness
i show others
and how little
i show myself.

grief leaves a taste
in my mouth
and i try to
swallow it
like shards
of broken glass
but you should know
it still settles
like dust
in my bones.

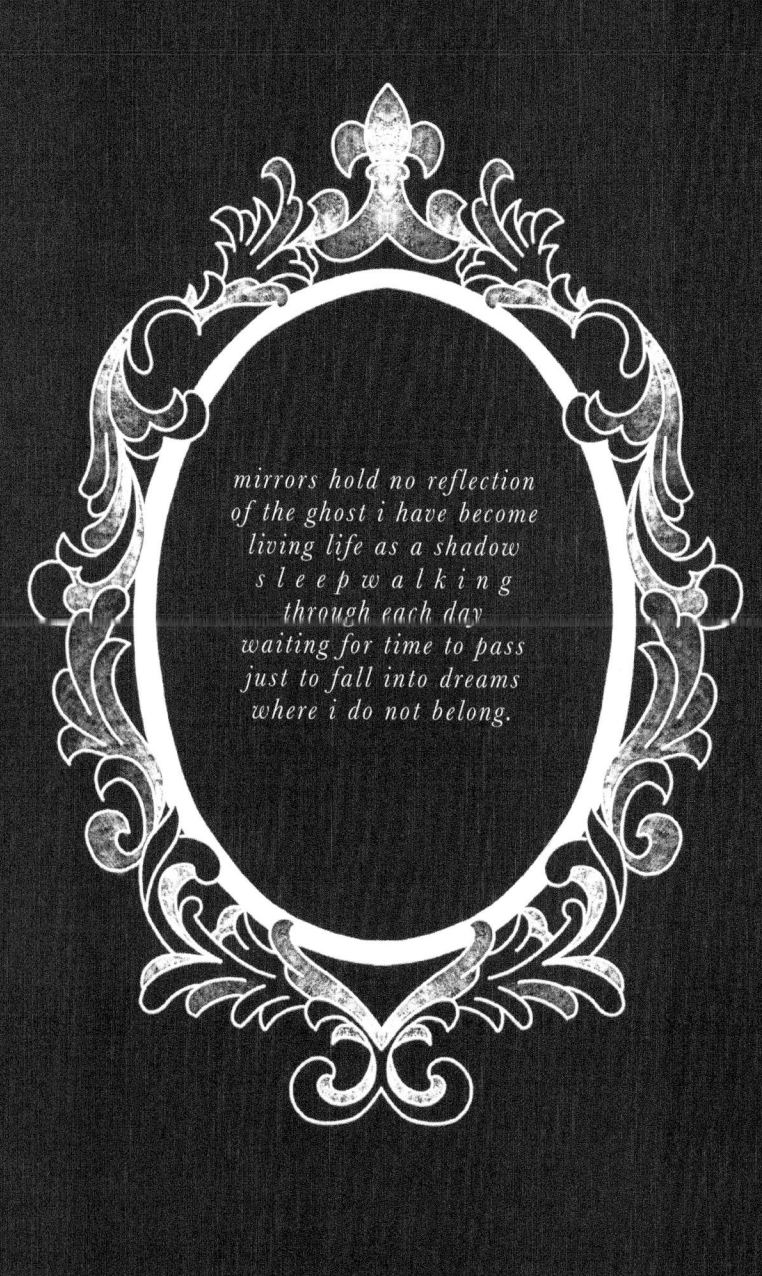

*mirrors hold no reflection
of the ghost i have become
living life as a shadow
s l e e p w a l k i n g
through each day
waiting for time to pass
just to fall into dreams
where i do not belong.*

i am trying so hard
not to run away in fear
from the happiness
i have always longed for
but i have never known
how to let the sun in
when all i ever wanted
was to keep the curtains closed.

i chase moonlight
as it walks on water
and i wonder if,
like me,
it is just an illusion –
a trick of the light.

because the ocean,
like me,
has a depth
that they
will never understand.

i am confined
to walls that know
my secrets
and air that will not
let me breathe.

you were lightning
across my darkening skies.

you were there
and then you weren't.

i watch them all
in glass jars
made of tinted rose
and i want to be
a part of it
and i never want
to be a part of it.

- from the outside looking in

i am trapped
in this cage
with walls
made of glass
but the transparency
is what makes it
impossible to bear.

- from the inside looking out

if the sky
were a little darker
and my heart
a little wiser
the stars
would shine brighter
and i wouldn't long
for you.

like the falling
autumn leaves
i knew you wouldn't stay
and like the fog
that blankets the trees
we were always meant to fade.

i am haunted
by the space
between us
and i am still
trying to find
my way back.

*i don't want to be
just another ghost
in your memory.*

i have been
counting the days
in raindrops
and dwelling so much
on the storms
that may or may not
fall on me tomorrow
that i didn't even notice
the sun shining today.

*i have lost so many todays
worrying about tomorrows.*

if you have
carved wounds
into their bones
please understand
you cannot simply
paint over them
with apologies.

i am burning
all the memories
of you.
it seems right
to end with fire
when that's how
it began.

i try to paint my world
how i want it
(my favourite colour is sunrise)

but the illness
wakes up with me
every morning
and like a robber
in the night
he stole the sun.

i cannot keep giving
all these pieces of me away.
i will still reach out to meet you
but only halfway.

there is silence.
and there always is
but tonight
the stillness of it all
feels out of place.

the focus has changed
and i stumble my way
through clouded vision.

it shouldn't be this quiet.
it shouldn't feel this empty.

i am a moth
in the dead of night
drawn to your flame
while searching for light
but as i try to fly closer
to seek what i yearn
my delicate wings
catch fire and burn.

it seems that
even the smallest cracks
can grow into
unmeasurable distance.

i have outgrown some.
others outgrew me
and i tried to shrink myself
to fill the gaps.

but in the quiet of it,
the distance grows and settles
and i am reminded
that there is no good
in goodbye.

you push me
under the water
and pull me back out
and i thank you
for saving me.

a haze of mist hides
an autumn morning
diluting the summer heat
the changing leaves
are falling
crisp under my feet.

melting amber skies
glisten like diamonds
through each
rust-coloured tree
in interwoven whispers
crackling in the breeze.

autumn passes fast
the air now bitter
the sun lower
in the sky
preparing for the winter
everything must die.

your hands were
hurting
from trying to hold
all of my pieces
together.

is that why
you let me go
like sand through
your fingers?

SABINA LAURA

i am waving goodbye,
chasing lights
out of car windows,
knowing that this may be
the last time
i lose my heart in a city
that never came back for me.

SABINA LAURA

the city lies awake
under a blanket of nostalgia.

i don't know if the lights
are waving hello or goodbye.

but i could never tell the difference
between beginnings and endings.

i sleep with my
windows open
but i am always
closing doors.
i think i hear
the walls whisper –
they are laughing
at my silence,
but i don't know
how to speak my truths
into existence
without them sounding
like apologies.

when you're pushed
underground
with the dirt

it's hard to tell
whether you've been planted
or buried.

we are creatures
of habit.

we hold on
like the mist that hugs
the trees at dawn

and we are always
trying to carry things
that do not let us grow.

how the flowers
hold different meanings
once they are picked and tied.

from the sweetest
i love you
to a final
goodbye.

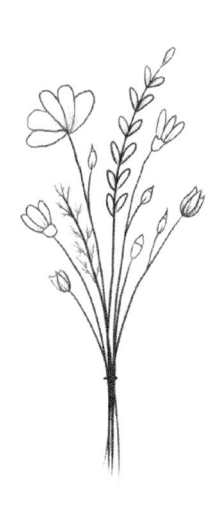

there is sand
in my toes
and wildflowers
in my hair
but there is
something missing
in my heart.
like the gentle sea breeze
i cannot hold onto you.
we have always been
oceans apart.

how the illness takes
and takes and takes.
so i cling to what is left
and hold it in my heart
even when i can no longer
hold it in my hands.

my words are snowflakes
melting instantly
or becoming
frozen echoes lost
amongst snow-covered trees.
because a silence hung
in the bitter air
before you left
filled with all the words
i didn't say.
*i didn't think i needed
to ask you to stay.*

i caught snowflakes
on my fingertips
but they melted
to my dismay.
i could not hold on
to something
that did not want
to stay.

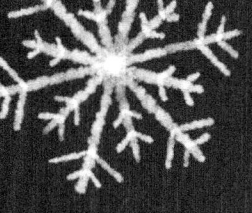

i bury my head
in the sand
until the tide
comes in
and i am left
with nothing
but truths
i didn't want
exposed.

like a dandelion,
my dreams get carried away
by the breeze

and i try
to catch them
all at once

but i have been
grasping with
the tips of my fingers,
not knowing
how to hold anything
completely.

i flip a coin to decide
which hurt more.

heads: i loved you.

tails: you didn't love me.

my heart has seen
many colours,
changing like the leaves,
falling into piles of hope
that didn't quite make it,
and stripped bare
like the trees
as autumn
comes to a close.

i am caged
like a bird
with no room
to spread my wings
but the hardest part
is that i still
remember
how to fly.

i close my palms
around these wounds
and when they become
too much to carry
i bury them
under anything i can.

the forest floor.
the bottom of the ocean.
even my own skin.

little did i know
that from the dirt
ghosts would grow.

you were
like the moon,
reminding me that
you do not
have to hold
something
to know how
to love it.

they tell me
open your eyes
and look up to the light.

but i have always
preferred a cloudy sky
with a chance of rain.

and sometimes
i want to disappear
in an eclipse
and hide behind the moon
like a sun afraid
of her own light,
but i have always
found it hard to believe
i could be more
than just a shadow
in the night.

i know
we grew apart
in silence
but i have
never
been good
at goodbyes.

watching the sun
rise again
over the rooftops
i whisper the things
i wish would come back, too.
like hope
like happiness
like you.

this body no longer
feels like a home.

it should be a safe space.

it has become a war zone.

i let everything into my heart
but i don't know how to let anything out
even when the weight of it
drags me down.
i wobble on tiptoes trying to reach
expectations that are too high.
i swear i try to touch the sky.
i still search for happiness
in places i only ever found pain
like a storm that can't let go of its rain.
and i let my heart break
so i know it was real,
so that even when i am empty
there is still something to feel.

i grow
from the rain
and let it hold me.
and some days,
when it taps
on my window
asking if it can cry
with me,
i say yes.
it is more honest
this way.

and when
something breaks
why do i always
collect together
all the broken shards
then wonder why
they make me bleed?

i spill my pain
onto parchment
and call it bravery
but sometimes there is
an honesty in this ink
that i cannot face.

she presses her face against the window
and the glass fogs like whispers
of a past that isn't coming back.

*these eyes don't want to let go
but my palms are already slipping.*

grow

SABINA LAURA

i will tell you a thousand times:
your first love should always be yourself.

when i fall
to the ground
you teach me
how to fly
with wings
i never knew i had.

when i break
you remind me
that these hands
are strong
and they can build
through the wreckage.

and when i cry
you tell me
that tears are not
a sign of weakness,
they show how
you survived.

i pick up courage
with my hands
not knowing
if they are strong enough
to hold it
and telling myself
over and over
that either way,
it will be okay.

don't let them tell you
it's weak to cry.

even the sky sheds tears
when the light has faded.

as these trees
come back to life
in the spring,
they whisper
a language
my heart is learning
and when they ask me
to come home
i will remind them,
remind myself,
i never left.

I

AM

LEARNING

TO

LET

GO

LIKE

AUTUMN.

I

AM

LEARNING

TO

GROW

LIKE

SPRING.

this storm in me needs time to rest
but i always find that healing
is more rain than sunshine.

i didn't know how to feel
without the sun on my skin
or how to feel alive
without the cold breeze
brushing against my cheeks
and i keep trying
to find my way back
but sometimes
we must make the choice
between holding on
and letting go.

i still look for the moon
even in daylight
and i said goodbye
to the darkness
like it will never return.

i smell citrus
and cinnamon
and the way things
f
      a
             l
                    l

like leaves.
bittersweet.

but they are only
preparing for winter.
the ultimate sacrifice for spring.
for something new to begin.

i save some grief for myself
even when others carry more of it.

which is to say,
the weight of pain
does not determine
how valid it is.

which is to say,
*you are entitled to hurt
even if others "have it worse".*

the sadness
comes in waves
creating ripples
in an ocean
threatening
to drown me.
but even if i sink,
i will make a home
at the bottom
of the sea
where all the
undiscovered
things live.

i will be
like the moon
and learn to shine
even when
i am not whole.

i belong
to the wildest shadows
and i am still searching
for the courage
to step out
into the moonlight.

i am more than
what tries to hold me back.

because even when
my feet can't carry me
as far as i would like,
i am learning how my voice
can take me to all the places
i never had a chance to miss.

you are the trees
that cannot keep
their promises
so they let go
until they become bare.

but i will be
the falling leaves
that do not care
where they land
and simply enjoy
breaking free.

and when it feels like
the world is ending
i remind myself that
sadness is a part of every story
no matter how many doors
we leave open behind us.

SABINA LAURA

even in these aching moments,
especially in these aching moments,
happiness finds me again
in the smallest ways.

i pull myself apart so often
i wonder how these pieces
still glue together.
but somehow, they do.
just not always
in their rightful places.
but even when
i am hurting,
i pick bullet wounds
out of my chest
and still love
with a full heart.

i have always
loved the rain too much
to chase sunshine
but even i see the beauty
in a new beginning
peeking over the horizon.

they told me
i wasn't enough wildfire
but when they are all burnt out
they will see me, still glowing,
the last flickering ember
amongst the devastation.

*i always knew how to burn
i just didn't know how to show it.*

i still carry
fragments
of a past life
like the last few leaves
on autumn trees
but when they finally fall,
they will make way
for better things.

i have rain in my eyes
spilling out in
droplets the size of tomorrow
but even if the weight of this
tries to pull me underwater
i will learn how to
rise and fall
with the waves.

*no storm will ever be
big enough to drown me.*

storms teach me
that not everything
should be held on to.
the clouds let go
when it becomes
too much to carry
and still create
something beautiful.

i want to take up
more space and less space
at the same time.
shrink myself to fit
in the corners
even sunlight can't reach.
build myself to fill
all the spaces
i shy away from.
perhaps the truth is
i just want to fit.

remember,
even when these tunnels
seem unending,
the light is never too far
out of reach.

i wear my heart
on my sleeve
and my honesty
like a crown.
i have rough edges
but a soft heart
and even through
all this darkness
i am always growing.

and when the weight
of the world
becomes too heavy
remember how kindness
will never be too much to carry.

why do you care so much
about what people think?
the storm does not worry
about where its rain
might fall. it will simply
let go.

i leave fingerprints on windows
as i chase raindrops
and footprints in the snow
on winter mornings.

i leave city lights in rear view mirrors
and memories inked in journals
telling stories of all the summers
that stole my heart,
at least for a little while.

i leave a fold
in all the pages of my story
i want to revisit someday
and a key under the mat
hoping someone will come back
to collect it.

because the truth is
i often leave
a part of me behind
never knowing ~~when~~ if
it might return
but that way i can promise
you will always know
where to find me.

i have forgotten to love
every single part of me
like a rainbow that didn't realise
she grew from the rain
just as much as the light.

she didn't love herself at seventeen
with her hair the colour
of autumn leaves
and freckles like constellations
painted on moon-kissed skin.

how i wish i could look back
through broken mirrors
and tell her that
she meant something.

the sky wore
a crown of lightning
while the clouds
had dry eyes.

but something had to give.

because sometimes
it takes letting go
to make space
for something new.

and then the rain fell.

my eyes feel heavy
like the sky in october
but my heart
is as colourful
as the leaves.

i put my ear
to the forest floor
listening for
the secrets
of the wild
because this pain
could cut through
to the centre
of the earth
but i will
get through
to the other
side.

and maybe my arms
have grown too tired
to hold this
but my eyes will
never stop searching
for miracles.

and when i
press my ear
to my pillow
i hear my heart
beating
just the same
as it used to.
i guess this is proof
that broken things
can still work.

i will always be grateful
for new beginnings
even when they mean
something has to end.

don't try to hold storms
in your hands.
the clouds were made to let go
and so were you.

and maybe
it would never
occur to you
or anyone else
to look beyond
what is right ahead
but i see the world
through curious eyes
that never stop asking
why.

i would like to
paint the sky
and walk
across the sea,
hold the moon
in my hands
and believe
i am free.

i feel it
returning
in waves
of black mist
but my eyes
will find a way
to see in the dark.

i promise myself
that my heart
will stay wild
even if my eyes
become cautious.

summer turned her back
all too soon and now
daylight withdraws
a little more every day.

but autumn is not a loss
when you have learnt
how to be evergreen.

for a while
i forgot that
i am my own home
but these walls
should not hold me back,
they should only
keep me safe.

it seems easier
to close my eyes
every time the sky
turns to smoky quartz

but somehow the light
always gets through

and i remind myself
that i am capable
of growing flowers from rain
and building mountains
from dirt.

i am tired
of my world
crashing down
at my feet every time
but i will build
something better
from all the pieces
left behind.

i thought growing up
meant finding my wings
but now i spend my days
trying to find a place to land.

we all have bruises
on our hearts
and flesh
scraped to the bone
but i want you to know.
you are so worth
the weight
of all of this.

the wild is always
changing
like a reminder.
you do not have to
be the same
to be beautiful.

you can run for miles
but the mountains will not seem any smaller.
if you climb them you will see the world
through the eyes of change.
i promise you the view is better from up here.

i hope you will
remember me
during violet nights
and dreamier days
and when i am afraid
to let go
at least i know
you are always
somewhere
under these stars.

IT

HURTS

TO

LET

GO

BUT

IT

HEALS

TO

BE

FREE.

you wrap yourself firmly
around every memory
like a snug blanket
on a cold night
and tangle your fingers
in my heartstrings
like thread holding together
a patchwork duvet.
but if you decide to let go
i think i might
u
  n
    r
      a
        v
          e
            l.

sometimes i stay awake
while the rest of the world is silent
counting stars while i wait
for dawn to approach
and as the sun appears
from behind the horizon
i know there is hope rising
with all this light.

sometimes change isn't needed,
but a different angle.

- *perspective is everything*

i look for forever
in temporary things
and i have watered
unforgiving things
with my tears
and maybe i will
always reach out
with open arms
but sometimes -
just sometimes -
they reach back
and take my hand.

a deep sleep
c o n s u m e s
me.

i live in the dark while
the rest of the world is shining.

but i think about
what lies on the edge
of tomorrow
when the sun
and the horizon reunite.

hope trickles in
like sunlight
through the cracks.

i will wake up soon and pray that
it won't be too late.

SABINA LAURA

bloom

it doesn't matter
where you were planted
or in which way
you grow.
all that matters is
you bloom.

i want to live in a world
where nobody is afraid
to fall in love
or admit it
and let love grow
like wildflowers
in the most unexpected
(but beautiful)
places.

i leave footprints
through the forest
but i don't need them
because as the stars
become soaked
in twilight
my lost heart
will follow them
home, instead.

i watch the sun
paint the world in gold
as another day
comes to a close.

i open all the windows
hoping the light
will reach me differently.

but the horizon
makes me a promise:
change is coming.

sometimes
i still wish
for home
but i am
finding peace
in being lost.

i want to create storms
that mean something
and let the wind carry me
somewhere new

because no matter how far i go
the wild will never leave my bones.

my heart
feels like spring
but i am finding
a way to let go.

even the blossom
falls from the trees.

from the rooftops
i dream in constellations
playing dot to dot
with the stars
because in a world that often
leaves me feeling
misunderstood
you make so much sense.

the night holds me
when i cannot sleep
and the sun forgot
to say goodbye.

i count stars
and the moon
sings lullabies.

and together
they tell me
that tomorrow
is waiting
around the corner
and it can be anything i want

if only i remember
to love it as much as the night.

i have a heart
that never wants to
follow my head
because it likes to run
wild and free
but all i ever wanted
was to know i was worth it
when my eyes were forgetful
and my hands had nothing to hold.

i count streetlights
out of car windows
and chase golden skies
during the evenings
i don't want to end
hoping i can keep
a piece forever
like pressed flowers
in forgotten pages.
but deep down i know
that all good things
come to an end.
it's how i remember
to be grateful for them.

i have constellations
mapped out across my heart
and stardust running
through my veins
and while darkness falls
on the rest of the world
my dreams keep me awake.

there is magic
in this.
in us.
in everything.
sometimes you just
have to look a little harder
to find it.

this paper thin skin
has always bruised easily
but when they tell me
to be brave,
i will remind them
that there is a
strength in softness
that doesn't need
to be heard
to be felt.

i have never known
which way i'm going
but no matter how lost i am,
the needle on the compass
will always end up
pointing north.

some things are left unsaid
and others get carried away
by the breeze through the forest.
and even if you feel
like your screams
get lost in the trees
i am still here.
i am still listening.

sometimes i get lost
in the forest
while the rest of the world sleeps.
but i don't mind.
you give me something
to come back to.

SABINA LAURA

i walk barefoot
across the sand
while holding sunbeams
in my hands.
i stare out into the horizon
and it keeps calling
the endless ocean
keeps on giving.
my eyes are lost
between shades of blue
but i know
i can paint the sky
any colour i choose.

i have braved
every storm i ever faced
with rain in my eyes
and thunder in my chest.

and i am weathered but stronger.
this will do less damage than the rest.

the sky seeped blood red
as day and night
shifted around us
splashes of colour
melting into one another
a lonely boat
just a mere silhouette
on the horizon
the peaceful water
glistening with the reflections
of the vivid sky above
as every drip
of orange and pink and gold
makes a promise
of something good
to be found in every day.

*the sky cried with me
and then showed me the sun.*

there is nowhere to hide at 3am
when everything is somehow
brighter in the darkness
and thoughts seem to tumble out
before we have a chance to
collect them.
but i am ready to fall
like a shooting star
because i no longer feel afraid.
and if you do,
look up to the sky.
it holds more secrets
than we ever could.

i have galaxies in my eyes
and stardust in my veins

and i am ready to build
a brand new universe.

i am ready to start again.

and although this life
may feel stained
black and white,
my eyes have always known
the colour of hope.

my heart roams in the wild.
a place where there is always
room to grow.

don't think i will stay
where they placed me.

i am all parts storm.

sometimes i cut the sky open
with my lightning.
sometimes i soothe the earth
with my rain.

either way
i am always moving.

i wondered
how the sun might feel
when she is hidden behind the clouds.

then i remember how i hide
behind my own skin
but it doesn't lessen my worth.

just like the sun.
she still shines bright
even if no one sees.

there are still parts of me
lost between the pages
i tried to erase
to disguise these wounds
and it seems that
frozen hearts linger
in the darkest places
but then again,
so does the moon.

i know you have secrets
your eyes are
brimming with them
fighting to escape
like the way
you came into this world
kicking and screaming.
so don't you see?
you were always
meant to be heard.

i carry home with me
in pockets i hope
have no holes
and hands i pray
won't slip.

i wear it under my skin
and feel it tangled up
in my hair.

so that even if i feel lost,
i can always find it
within me.

i still believe
in fairytales
like the dreamer i am
and i am always
lost in thought
or with my head
in the clouds.
i dream with
eyes open
so the darkness
cannot get in
and i put my faith
in words -
they're the only
magic we need.

i know
that there are
constellations
hidden in
your soul
and i want
to get lost
in them
in every way
i know.

summer left
before she said goodbye
but the september moon
is waiting for me
and there is still
so much room to grow
under her light.

as the sun
wakes the earth

light peeks in
through the window

and the walls are
flecked in sunlight

a gentle reminder
that although most things
will end,

everything will begin.

i never knew
how to carry
something as heavy
as hatred.
how can you fly
being held down
by its weight?
forgiveness is
as light as a feather
and my wings
are made of
thousands of them.

i open my curtains
to ever changing skies
but i fall in love
with all of them
and it takes time
to be gentle with yourself
when storms loom
on the horizon
but i am grateful
for the way
everything shines
so much brighter
after being in the dark
for so long.

i could trace
each line on an atlas
a thousand times
and hold a compass
in my hands
but i will still get lost.

my head is always
in the clouds
but i have never been
afraid of heights.

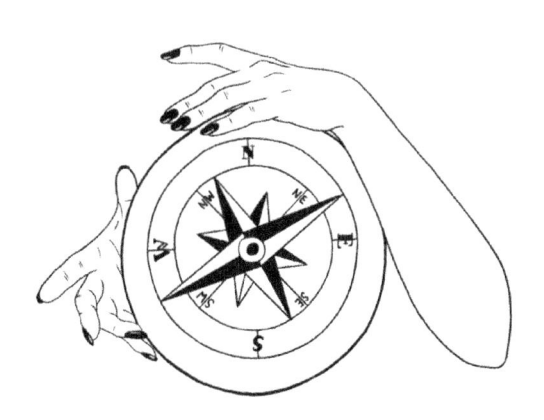

under this
evening sky
the light is fading
but i promise,
my light will not dim.
and these autumn leaves
are changing
but i promise,
so am i.

i am not telling you
that the light
will stop all darkness.
but as the moon
plays hide and seek
amongst the clouds,
i am telling you that
even in darkness
there will always be light.

gradually, it heals
like a week-old bruise
that only hurts
when you press it.
it's like pulling splinters
out of your skin.
as soon as they're out
you forget the pain.
it is dusting off cobwebs
that don't belong
because they only cloud
your vision.
and it is a promise
that one day,
the end
will start to feel
like the beginning.

i am always shifting like the clouds
and i will not be sorry
when i let go of my rain.

some things just aren't meant to stay.

i'm afraid
you'll be disappointed
if you're looking
for a rose
because i have
wildflowers growing
through my skin
with roots deep
in my bones.

the air that settles
in my tired lungs
feels foreign now.

my heart
hangs heavy
within bruised ribs.

i have shed my skin
more times
than i remember.

but my veins
keep pumping this blood
around and around.

and i am still here
underneath it all.
different,
but the same.

i remind myself
over and over
that a bad day
is just a drop of water
in an ocean.
so even when
it feels like
i am drowning,
i still hold on to tomorrow.
i find a way to start again.
i always start again.

i find comfort in the shadows
where silence goes unnoticed.
they don't tell me
i should be somewhere else.
and i'm not afraid
of the dark anymore,
because even if the sun isn't,
the moon will always be
on my side.

i find hope
in all the places
i need it most.

i know that you will, too.

these poems grow
from a garden of words in my head
and for a while i forgot
that flowers need rain to grow
and new seeds cannot be planted
if dead roots are in the way.

so i rip them out and start again
and now flowers bloom through my skin
because beautiful things
can grow from the dark
and i am one of them.

i am made up of
daydreams and nightmares
and i count stars
instead of sheep
when i can't sleep.
and when the clock
strikes 11:11
or a dandelion shivers
in the breeze,
i make a wish
because i will never believe
in anything less than magic.

my heart changes
like the wild.

it wilts.
it grows.
it blooms.

i am a moonflower.
i will bloom
even when it's dark.

*thank you for giving
my words a home.*

*follow on social media:
@sabinalaurapoetry*

Printed in Great Britain
by Amazon